CELTIC

BODY art

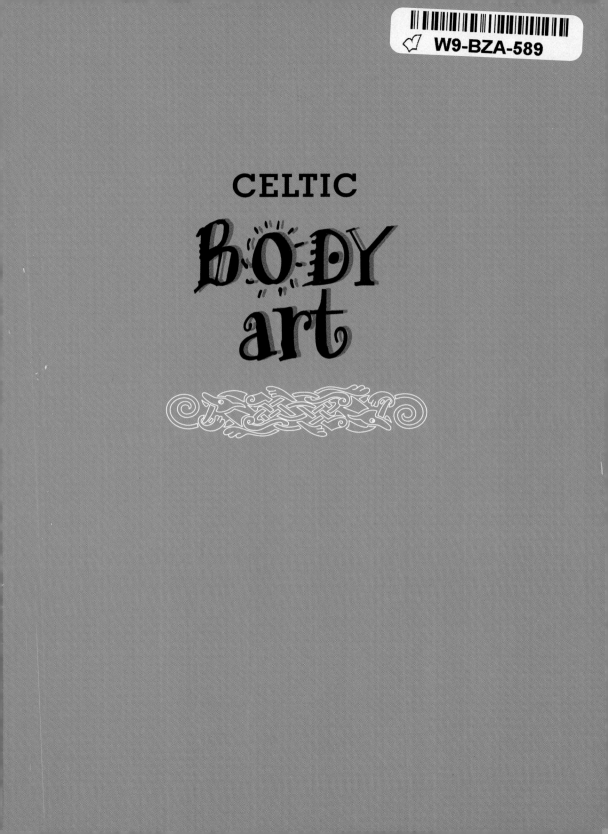

CELTIC

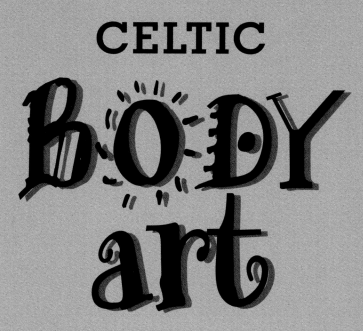

BODY

art

AILEEN MARRON

in association with Halawa Henna

Photography by Emma Peios

JOURNEY
EDITIONS

'One must be a work of art, or wear a work of art'
OSCAR WILDE

First published in the United States in 1999 by Journey Editions, an imprint of Periplus Editions (HK) Ltd., with editorial offices at 153 Milk Street, Boston, Massachusetts 02109.

The catalog card number is on file with the Library of Congress

ISBN 1-885203-78-0

DISTRIBUTED BY:

USA
Tuttle Publishing Distribution Center
Airport Industrial Park
364 Innovation Drive
North Clarendon, VT 05759-9436
Tel: (800) 526-2778
Tel: (802) 773-8930

JAPAN
Tuttle Shokai Ltd.
1-21-13, Seki
Tama-ku, Kawasaki-shi
Kanagawa-ken 214-0022, Japan
Tel: (044) 833-0225
Fax: (044) 822-0413

First Edition
05 04 03 02 01 00 99   1 3 5 7 9 10 8 6 4 2

AN EDDISON•SADD EDITION
Edited, designed and produced by
Eddison Sadd Editions Limited
St Chad's House, 148 King's Cross Road
London WC1X 9DH

Phototypeset in Garamond ITC by BT and Geometric Slab BT using QuarkXPress on Apple Macintosh.
Origination by Bright Arts PTE, Singapore
Printed and bound by C & C Offset Printing Co. Ltd, Hong Kong

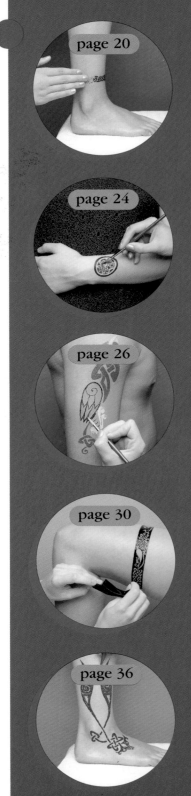

page 40

page 44

page 48

page 52

page 56

Contents

introduction

This book shows you how to create ten fantastic Celtic designs, and gives you the inspiration to create many, many more.

Celtic designs look great as tattoos, and all the main styles of Celtic artwork are covered here, including interlacing knotwork, spiral and 'key' patterns, and zoomorphic designs (these include bird and animal shapes as an integral part of the design). The knotwork is probably the most recognized of all the styles, and you will see that it features in most of the tattoo designs included in this book.

Many of the designs I've chosen to use here date back to the Picts – the 'pre-Celts' who lived in northern Britain, and whose style of artwork went on to become the hallmark of Celtic style. For example, 'key' patterns – angular maze-like configurations of lines – were particularly well-known, and Pictish adaptations of animals and birds depicted elongated bodies, legs, wings, necks or tails, often becoming part of a knotwork or spiral pattern.

You will find that some of the tattoo designs in this book are delicate and sophisticated, while others are more bold, daring and colourful. You can coordinate your body art with your clothing and the occasion – so if you're off to a party why not go for something really bold and bright, like the Celtic winged creature on page 26, or the mythological waistband on page 48? For something more understated you could choose a classic design like the ankle bracelet on page 20, or the knotwork collar on page 44. You'll also find that the different products used suit different occasions, too.

Celtic tradition

Ancient books from the Celtic era depict fantastic examples of the Celts' intricate style of artwork. The *Book of Kells* is perhaps the most famous, and a beautiful detail from this book is shown opposite. The brilliance of the designs from this era is perhaps difficult to associate with the historic account of the Celts, which paints them as an uncivilized and barbaric people. But body art played an important role for the Celts, particularly in battle: they used it to change their appearance in order to shock and intimidate the enemy. The blue coloration that they applied to their skin (traditionally thought to have been created using woad, a plant whose leaves yield a blue dye) made them  appear fearsome, and also made them feel more confident.

Today, Celtic body art is obviously not worn for quite the same reasons, but it still has the same striking effect!

Detail from the Book of Kells, Eire

introduction

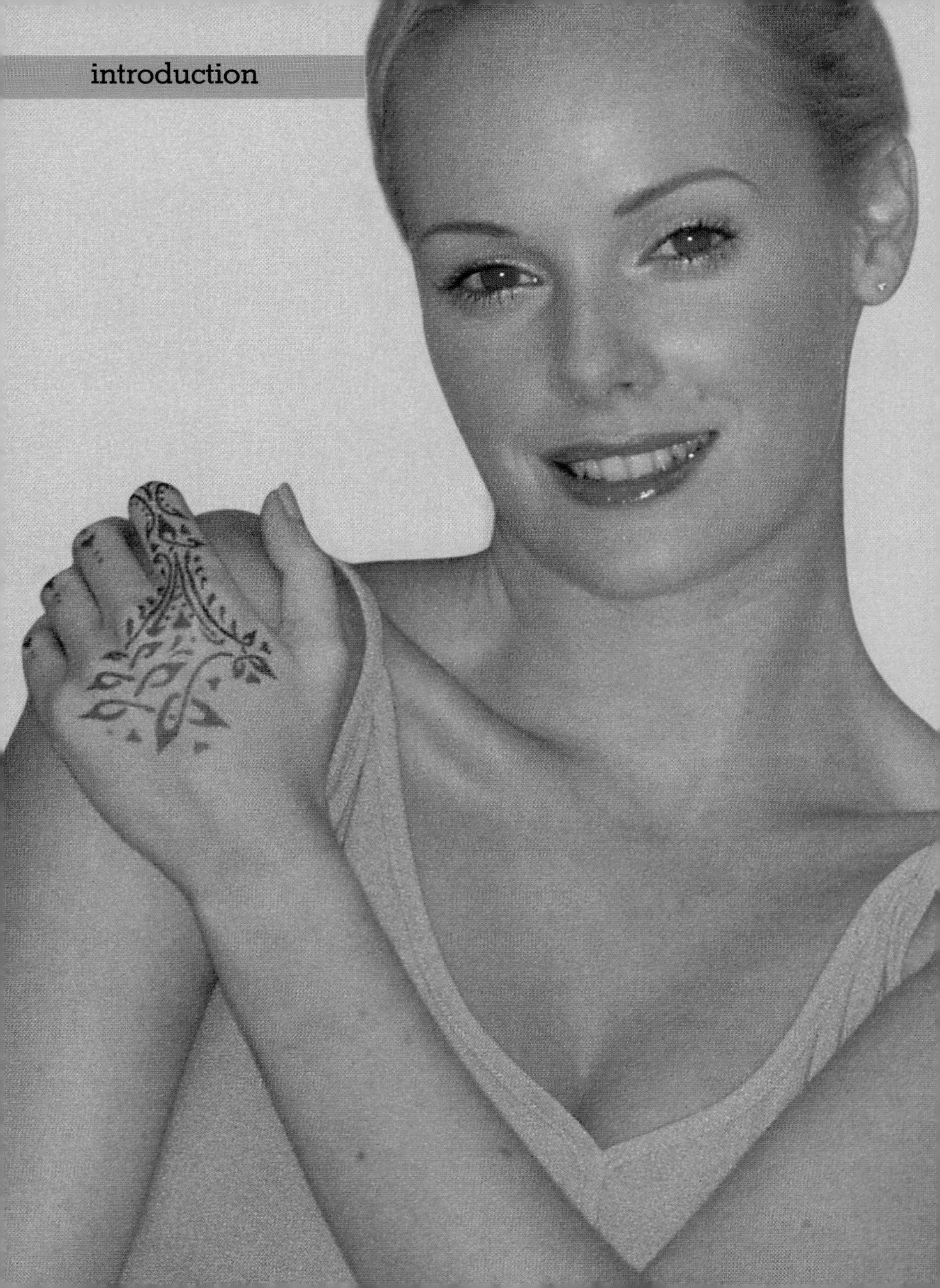

getting started

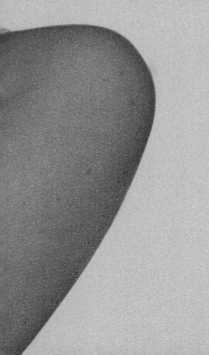

There are many products you can use for body art. In this book I look at traditional henna, body paints, cosmetic inks and dyes, and show you the techniques you will need to use to get the very best effects from each. All these products are easy to get hold of *(see Useful Contacts, page 62)*.

Take a look at the ten designs in the book. They may look intricate, but all can be broken down into simple, repetitive steps. Choose the medium you want to use and try out the techniques demonstrated *(see pages 12–19)*. Start off with one of the simpler designs early in the book, like the knotwork anklet *(page 20)* or the Pictish circle *(page 24)*. Many of the designs have transfers which give you something to follow and help get you on your way, so you can create beautiful body art from day one. As you progress, move on to the more complex freehand designs later in the book – try mixing and matching products for some amazing effects. The design outlines are clearly shown for you to copy out. You can always skip the tricky bits until you get more practice. Remember – the designs are up to you. You can just copy them as they are, or copy elements of one design and add your own freehand motifs – or perhaps combine patterns from different designs. And why not try them on different body locations as well – the possibilities are endless!

Before you know it you will be mastering the techniques and designing your very own temporary tattoos. So call your friends round and get practising on each other straight away!

henna techniques

Henna body art uses a long-lasting and natural product. Fashionable in the East for thousands of years, it has finally made it to the West. Follow the preparation instructions with your henna (see Useful Contacts, page 62, for suppliers). Once prepared, henna paste is most effectively applied by piping it onto the skin, as you would squeeze icing through a tube. Henna stains the skin permanently, the design disappearing as the body regenerates its epidermis, about every 2–4 weeks. Henna will stain the skin a reddish-brown colour (the exact shade varies). *(For more information on henna, see Further Reading, page 63.)*

Catalyst solution is mixed with the henna powder

Henna powder

Mehlabiya oil is applied to the skin first to aid henna development

don't forget!

- Cleanse skin first and apply mehlabiya oil
- Leave design uncovered until dry
- Wait another hour before brushing off dry paste
- Don't get design wet for 12 hours
- Design takes 48 hours to develop full colour
- Design lasts 2–4 weeks

fine lines ▶

Holding the cone near the tip, squeeze the henna onto the skin. Use even pressure for an even line. Drag the tip across the skin from side to side, or from top to bottom as needed, moving the cone away from the direction of the flow of henna paste.

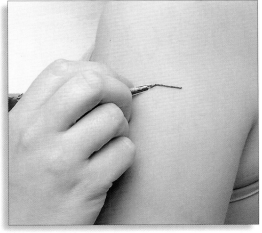

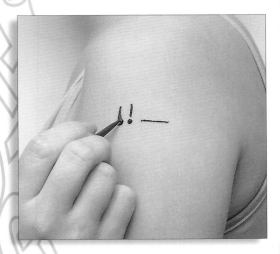

◀ pressure

Apply a small line with a dot underneath, then repeat this without the break, gradually increasing the pressure on the cone as you reach the large end. You can also start at the large end and work backwards.

block fill ▶

Use rows of straight lines to fill in large areas. Remember that it is only the paste in contact with the skin that will stain, but don't worry about build-up on the skin – it is unavoidable. Don't try to spread product on the skin – you will remove more than you spread!

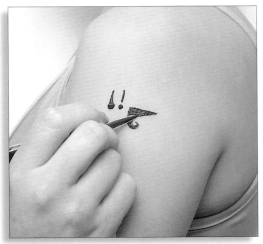

body-paint techniques

There are two main types of body paints available: grease and water-based. Both come in an array of colours. You don't need to keep adding water to grease paints, so they are quite quick to use, making them popular in theatres and with face painters. I like water-based paints more, though. I find application smoother and I like the fact that you can wash them off clothes! You can achieve a great number of effects with body paints, from basic backgrounds to detailed designs.

Grease body paints

don't forget!

- Cleanse skin first
- Set paint with talcum powder
- Use warm water and soap to remove water-based paints
- Use cleanser or baby oil to remove grease paints
- Designs last about 1 day

Cosmetic sponges for blending paint

Water-based body paints

Paintbrushes in a range of sizes

fine lines ▶

Using just a little body paint on the tip of a brush, rest your hand on the arm and apply a smooth line. Use the length of the brush as a guide for your line. When painting a long line, apply a small section at a time to keep control.

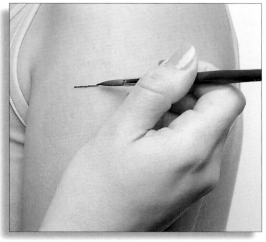

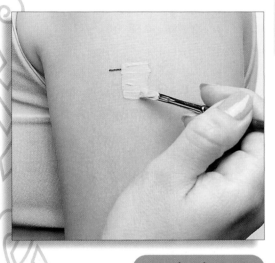

◀ block fill

Body paints dry very quickly, so you can apply a different colour over the first almost immediately. You can also apply a light colour over a dark one, so you don't have to plan the order of colour application. If you're filling in a large area, load your brush quite well.

texture ▶

You can create great paint effects using wet and dry sponges. Try applying wet paint in circular motions for a smooth background, or dabbing and smudging on finishing touches with a dry sponge – as I have here, with a shimmering silver.

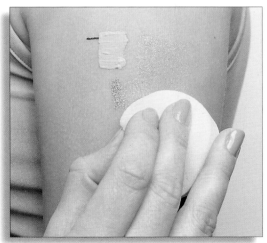

body-dye techniques

Cosmetic dyes can be hard to find in the shops. *(See Useful Contacts, page 62 to locate a good source.)* The dyes used in this book have been specially formulated to act like henna paste. However, Mother Nature is still the best because these coloured dyes last for 2–4 days, unlike henna which is a longer lasting cosmetic dye. Dying the skin creates the most realistic tattoo effect: no product is left on the skin, so there is no light reflection and hence detection.

Activator must be applied to the skin first

Body dyes come is a wide range of colours

Paintbrush for shading effects

don't forget!

- First cleanse skin and apply activator liquid
- Peel off dye when dry
- Designs last 2–4 days (waterproof spray will prolong their life)
- Remove with warm water and soap – will take about 7 washes

shading ▶

The gel-like dye can be mixed on the skin during application. Here I applied a yellow circle and then mixed blue directly into the still-wet product, gradually adding less blue as I neared the top left. After drying, the colour will gradually fade from yellow through to dark green.

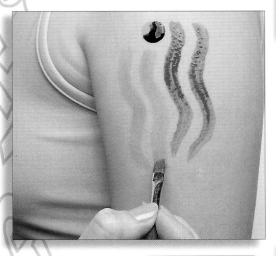

◀ brush work

Dyes can also be applied using a brush. Paint it on in its gel form, or water it down in a palette to paint lighter shades of the same colour. Here I've applied the product in gel form and *(far left)* in a very diluted form, illustrating the shading capabilities.

pressure ▶

Follow the henna instructions *(see page 13)*. Dye doesn't need as much pressure to force it out of the cone though. Once the product has dried (20–40 minutes), use your hand to gently rub the dry film away, revealing the temporary stain beneath.

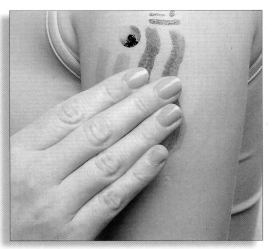

cosmetic-ink techniques

All of us have used ink to draw on ourselves at sometime, whether just jotting down a phone number, or creating masterpieces as children. You must make sure, though, that you use a cosmetic ink (also known as temporary tattoo paint). The skin is a living organ and I recommend that all products you use on it are designed for the purpose. There are lots of cosmetic pens and inks available. Personally, I prefer the alcohol-based bottled inks that you apply with a brush. They dry very quickly and leave a clean edge (I find the 'felt-tip' kind tend to let the colour bleed around the edges of a design).

Alcohol-based cosmetic inks

Paintbrushes in a range of sizes

don't forget!

- Cleanse skin first
- Set ink with talcum powder
- Inks are waterproof – you need alcohol swabs or oil-based cleansers to remove them
- Designs will last 2–5 days

fine lines ▶

Use a fine brush, and follow the same instructions as when using body paint *(see page 15)*. You will need to keep an alcohol-based cleanser close at hand to keep the tip of your brush clean and free from residual product build-up.

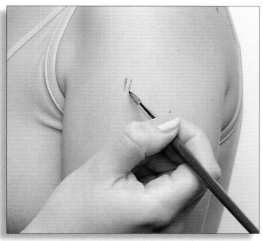

◀ block fill

Again, follow the instructions on page 15. You'll notice that a lighter-coloured ink will not cover a darker one, but will change colour slightly according to the colour applied on top. Here the fine blue lines now appear green.

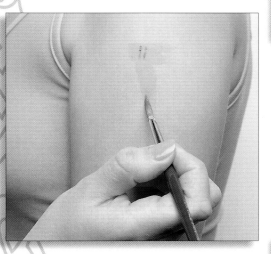

mixing ▶

You can achieve some great effects if you mix colours on the skin. These inks are quite fast-drying, so you have to be quick and confident. I applied yellow from a loaded brush and then almost immediately began to add blue in vertical streaks.

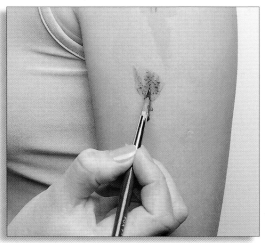

knotwork anklet

An intricate design built up using simple repetitive stages

Natural henna paste has been used here to create a classic design. The knotwork style is a well-known form of Celtic artwork, derived from the *Book of Durrow*. The continuous intertwining of the design symbolizes eternity.

◄ one

Apply a thin layer of mehlabiya oil to the ankle using cotton wool. The band of glistening oil will give you a guide for the transfer application. Now you need to cut out the transfers.

two ►

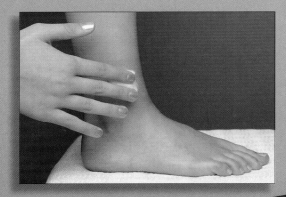

Three transfers are used for this design. First select the transfer with the solid vertical line on the left edge and, starting at the left-hand side, firmly press it against the skin and then peel it away.

▼ three

Then use the transfer with the 'open' links at both ends to print the outline repeatedly around the ankle. Try to match up the links as best you can. To finish off the design, apply the transfer with the solid line on the right edge.

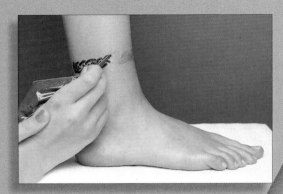

▲ four

Holding the henna cone near the tip, start to fill in the outline. Start at the left-hand side of the design and work round the ankle (if you are left-handed, work from right to left).

▲ five

To avoid smudging, move around the ankle, instead of asking your model to move. Continue filling in the outline, making sure you leave large enough gaps to make the knotwork stand out.

Leave it to dry (20–40 minutes depending on room temperature) and an hour later brush off any remaining henna paste to reveal an orange design. Don't get it wet for 12 hours, and 48 hours later you will have a rich brown tattoo that can last for up to 4 weeks. This design looks great round the upper arm, too.

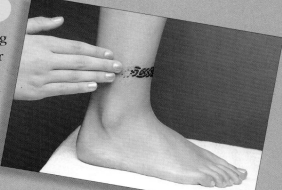

Pictish circle

A striking design created with simple freehand techniques

Cosmetic ink has been used to apply this angular pattern based on 'key' designs created by the ancient Picts – the *Book of Lindisfarne* illustrates many examples. Key patterns are great to start freehand work with. Try the simple one shown below first, then try copying the design to the right.

one ▶

Cleanse the skin using an alcohol swab. Using a little ink on the tip of a brush, paint a circle outline. A good way to create a circle is to paint small dots onto a roll of tape and then stamp it onto the wrist, as I've done here. This gives you a basic guide for the circle.

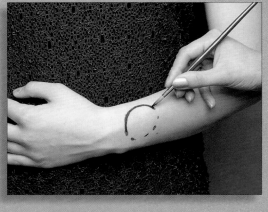

◀ two

Again, using a little ink on the very tip of a brush, paint in the basic maze design. Start in the centre of the circle and paint the two short parallel lines, then paint the long vertical lines at a 90-degree angle to these, and continue like this.

▼ three

Paint block areas of ink wherever there is enough room. Use the surrounding lines as a guide for each shape. To set the design, rub in plenty of talcum powder. The tattoo should last for 2–5 days.

winged creature

A colourful design created using freehand brushstrokes

Water-based body paints have been used here to create this colourful, vibrant design. It is based on an animal-like interpretation of a bird from the *Book of MacRegol,* although the bird here is much bigger with less complicated detail, making it easier to apply freehand. Use the outline printed on the page as a guide to copy from. For ideas for other colours and a different wing design, refer to the picture on page 2.

one ▶

Using a well-loaded brush, paint on the basic wing shape and then fill in the top and bottom sections, painting in the triangular edges. Then clean the brush and fill in the centre of the wing in green, painting right up to the orange edge and over the orange outline.

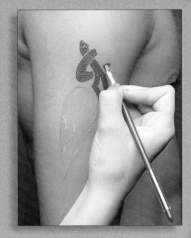

◀ two

Using blue paint, apply the neck of the bird and then the knot. Paint on thin sketch lines first, and then paint over these lines one section at a time to make them thicker.

three ▶

Next, paint in the beak using yellow. Use the blue lines as a guide to 'fit' the beak into. Then paint the rest of the head in orange, again using the beak and the blue lines as a guide to help you 'fit' the head.

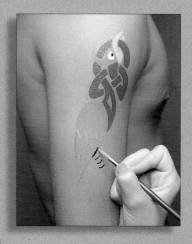

◀ four

Add the final blue section above the head, then create an eye using black and white paint. Next, paint on the leg in orange, starting at the green part of the wing. Then, using only the tip of the brush and a little paint, apply the black lines on the leg and wing.

◀ five

Using yellow again, paint in the foot – use the shape of the leg and wing to guide you *(see outline above)*. Use gold paint when adding the talons, then blue paint for the knotwork tail. Finally, use black to paint the spiral on the wing and finish the outline.

six ▶

Liberally apply talcum powder and rub it in to dry and set the design. The tattoo will last until you wash it off. If you have used water-based paints you can remove it using warm water and soap, but with grease paints you'll need to use cleanser or baby oil.

zoomorphic garter

An intricate design created using transfers and basic filling techniques

Cosmetic dyes have been used here to create this intricate design. The pattern is only slightly different to the original version depicted in the *Book of Kells,* where many examples of interlacing birds can be found. This design works beautifully as a band, and its length makes it particularly ideal for a garter, though it looks good as an armband, too. The tattoo will last for 2–4 days, but you can prolong its life by using a waterproof spray. The dye will wash out after 6–7 washes with warm water and soap.

one ▶

Apply activator around the thigh and rub it in. This design uses two transfers – first, press the longer one against the thigh, using one hand to secure it and the other to pat it down to ensure that all of the outline transfers. Then peel it away and press on the shorter transfer, aligning the curved line over the 'wing' shape already printed.

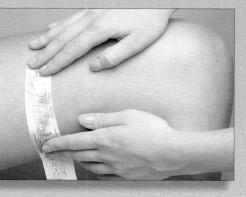

▲ two

Peel away the shorter transfer and apply both transfers again (or as much as you need) on the other side of the thigh, to take the design right around the leg to complete the garter.

three ▼

Holding the cone near the tip, start to fill in the knotwork in the design with orange dye. You don't need a lot of pressure as the design is very delicate. Make sure you leave enough room between the lines to keep the knotwork clear and visible.

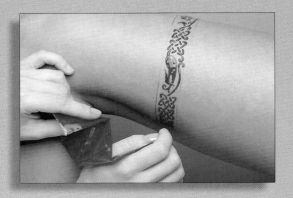

◄ four

Continue to apply the orange dye around the thigh, filling in the birds as you go. If it gets difficult to work underneath the thigh, you can continue with your friend standing up with her legs straight.

five ►

Leave the orange dye to dry for around 20–40 minutes (depending on room temperature) and then gently peel it away from the skin, revealing the orange design. Always remember to apply the light-coloured dye first – this prevents it from bleeding into the darker colour.

◄ six

Using a dark blue-black dye, now fill in the surrounding area. Be careful when you do this, as you don't want to cover over the orange design that you have just done.

▼ seven

Continue filling in the dark dye all around the leg, making sure that both ends of the band have a clean edge. Once all the filling is done, you are ready to add the final touches.

◀ eight

Finally, add details to the birds by applying a freehand pattern on the wings. Use the shape of the wing to guide you, and be careful not to smudge the dye that you have just applied, which will still be drying.

◀ nine

Leave the dark dye to dry naturally for a strong colour (such as shown on page 61) or fast-dry it with heat for a paler shade. Then peel it away to reveal the finished design.

interlaced birds

An elaborate design created using both freehand and symmetrical techniques

Natural henna has been used here to create this bold design. The design is adapted from a piece of jewellery thought to have been created using ancient Celtic references, and reflects the zoomorphic artwork style so popular throughout Pictish and Celtic art. It also noticeably features the ancient-style spirals inside the birds' wings, as well as the familiar knotwork. For a different look, you could also use the transfer on its own to create a striking tattoo on your back or your shoulder.

Using cotton wool or a brush, apply a thin layer of mehlabiya oil onto the foot and ankle (you will need to go quite far up the leg). Press the transfer against the foot and then peel it away.

▼ **two**

Following the transfer outlines, start to fill in the design. Pay special attention to the birds' heads when applying the henna, making sure that you don't fill in the gaps by mistake.

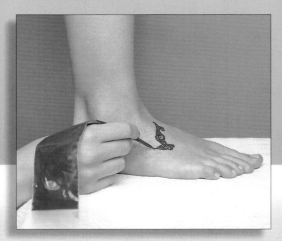

◀ three

Start the freehand section by continuing the line from the design right up the ankle, keeping the line at the same angle. Stop when you have just crossed the centre line of the leg.

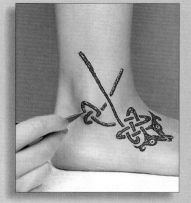

◀ four

You can apply the knot beneath the ankle bone freehand, or cut out one of the knots from the transfer you have already used. If you use the transfer, make sure you join up the two lines at the point on the right-hand side of the knot.

◀ five

Carry on applying the henna freehand, and branch off another line to create the basic wing shape. Then draw the spirals, and apply the tapering points for the wing tips above the spirals.

▲ six

Fill in the wings using lines of henna, leaving the spiral gaps clear, and finally apply the feet. Leave the henna to dry before you brush it off, revealing the design.

Celtic fighting dog

A complex, bold design created freehand

Cosmetic inks have been used here for this typically colourful design. It's an example of the popular Ancient British Fighting Dog featured throughout the *Book of Kells.* Designs like this traditionally feature as part of an illustration telling a story.

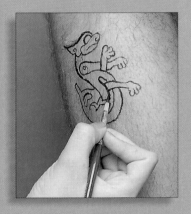

◀ one

Copy the outline of the body, using only a little black ink to ensure fine lines. Start with the head – the mouth and nose first – then the top of the head and ear, on down to the neck. Each part will guide you to the next stage. Then do the spiral at the top of the shoulder, carrying on down the spine, and paint the third leg down so that you can paint the stomach. Continue until the body is complete.

two ▶

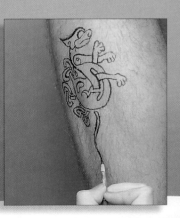

If you're feeling confident, you can paint on a fourth leg *(see outline above right)* but you might find it easier just to paint three to start off with, as I've done here. Next, paint the three knots along the left-hand side. Start with the top one and work down – always paint the lines shorter than you think necessary to make sure you have room for the gaps. Finally, paint the tail – you can taper it to a point, or paint a spiral at the end *(see outline)*.

three ▶

Paint the colours into the eye (white and blue are used here), cleaning your brush with alcohol in between. You can rest your hand on the design, as the ink dries very quickly.

Celtic fighting dog

◀ **four**

Using a well-loaded brush, fill in the rest of the design with purple ink. Don't worry too much if you go outside your black outline as you can always use an alcohol swab to remove any mistakes.

five ▶

Using the light blue ink again, go back to the top of the design and paint in some highlights. This will give your design more presence.

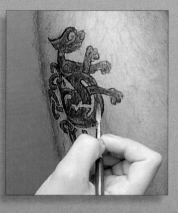

Once you have finished, dust the design with talcum powder and rub it in to set and dry the design. The ink is waterproof, and the design should last for around 2–5 days. If you want to remove it sooner, use alcohol swabs or oil-based cleansers.

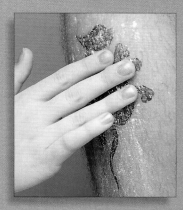

knotwork collar

A *delicate design created using basic knotwork and symmetry*

This beautiful design, based on an example of Pictish knotwork by George Bain, was created using cosmetic dye. Instead of following the traditional Celtic style of filling in the background shape, I have filled in the knotwork to give the design a more delicate feel, ideal for its location.

◄ one

Rub activator into the skin, covering the entire area of the design, then firmly press the transfer onto the skin. Use the middle of the collarbone as a guide to position your transfer.

two ►

Holding the cone near the tip, start to apply the cosmetic dye. I've mixed some colours here to create a fashionable khaki colour. Start at the left-hand side of the design to avoid smudging, and fill in the whole of the transfer outline.

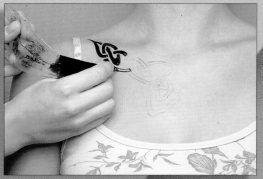

knotwork collar

three ▶

Once you have filled in the first half, cut a piece of tracing paper to size and gently place it onto the still-wet design, which will hold it in place. Using the same dye, quickly apply fine sketch lines over the design showing through the tracing paper.

four ▶

Then lift up the tracing paper and flip it over, pressing it onto the other side of the chest, so that the sketched lines leave an outline for you to follow as a guide for the rest of the design. Carry on applying the dye, working from the centre of the chest towards the right-hand side.

◀ five

When you've finished, go back to the start of the second half and touch up the line work, making sure all the lines have smooth edges and are the same width as the first half of the design. Leave it to dry for 20–40 minutes before you peel off the dry dye to reveal the subtle colour of the design.

mythological waistband

A stunning design combining transfers and freehand work

Again, cosmetic dye is used to achieve this vibrant blue design. This example of Pictish zoomorphic artwork incorporates the mythological 'Beast' with mathematical knotwork unique to the Picts. The location of this tattoo is daring and fun, but it also looks good as an armband.

one ▶

Rub activator on the stomach, covering the entire area of the design. Press the transfer firmly onto the left-hand side of the stomach, using the navel as the centrepoint to line up the transfer.

◀ two

Peel the transfer away and rotate it, turning it upside down. Press it down onto the right-hand side of the stomach, taking care to line it up with the transfer print you've already done.

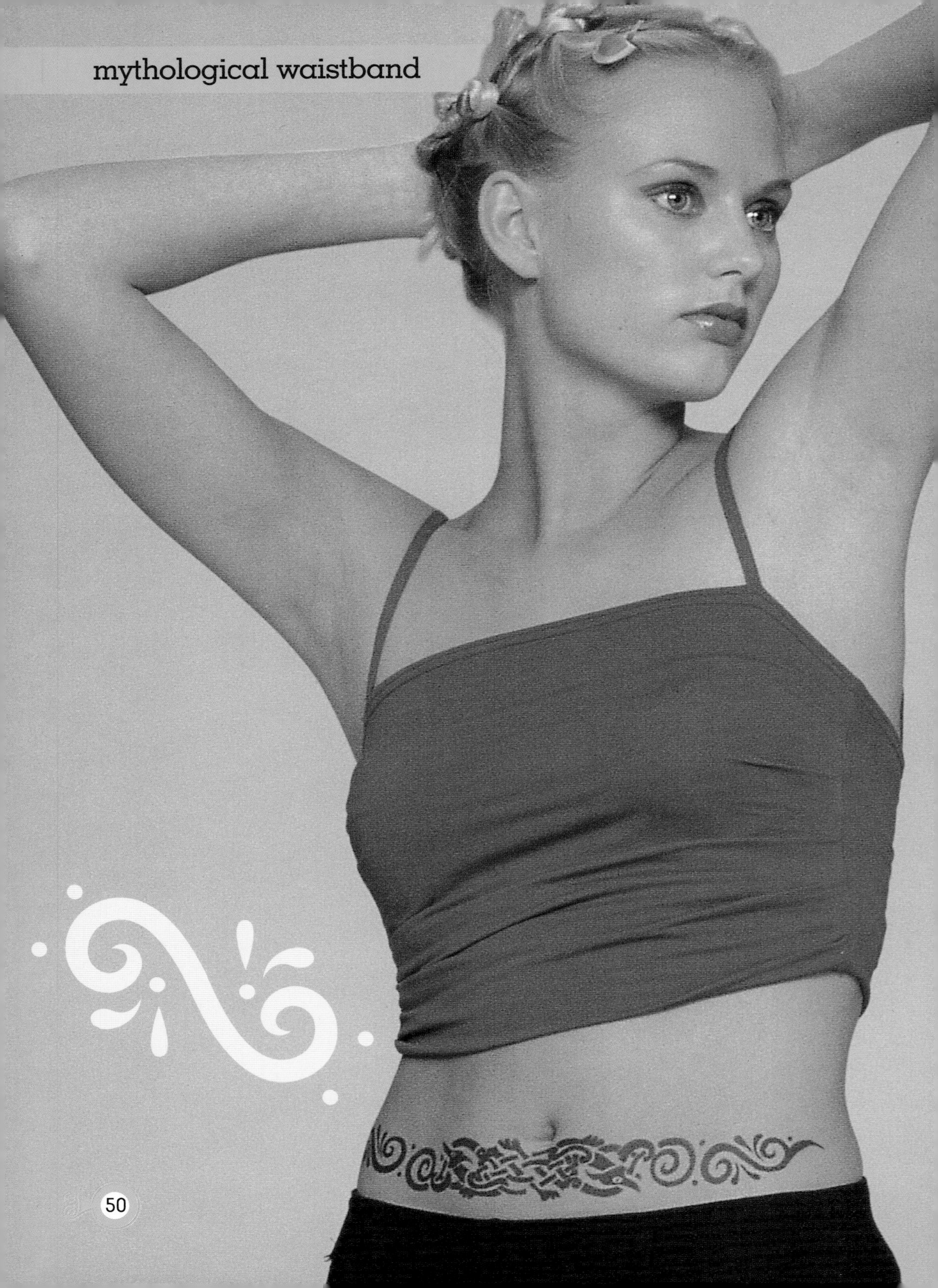

three ▶

Fill in the first half of the design, holding the cone near the tip, taking care to leave all the gaps in the design knotwork clear.

◀ four

Continue filling in the outline across the stomach. This design takes quite a while to apply, so you should stop now and again to let your friend move around!

five ▶

Go back to the left-hand side and apply the freehand section to elongate the design (copy the motif opposite). Start in the centre of the spiral and work outwards, applying the dots and teardrops to finish.

◀ six

Now repeat this freehand section on the right-hand side to complete the design. Leave it to dry, and then peel off the dye, revealing a striking blue Celtic tattoo.

body armour

A *bold design built up using two freehand brushwork techniques*

A combination of body paint and cosmetic ink has been used to create this stunning piece of body art. Once again, Pictish 'key' patterns form the basis – examples of similar designs can be found in other ancient cultures, from Central American to Egyptian.

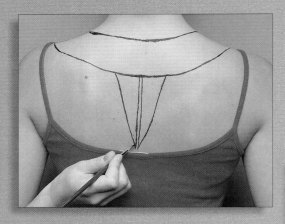

◁ one

Use a small amount of body paint on the tip of a brush to paint on the basic outline of collar and 'daggers'. Your outline doesn't have to be perfect on the inside, because the bronze paint will go over it.

two ▷

Use a well-loaded brush to fill in the entire design with bronze paint. Use long strokes to get even coverage, and try to even out the black outline when you paint up to it with the bronze.

body armour

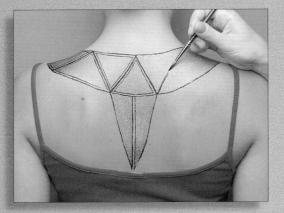

▲ three

Using only a little black ink, paint in the zig-zag line and the inner triangles as you go. Paint the middle triangle first, and use the width of the daggers to guide you. The bronze paint will dry straight away, so there's no need to wait before painting the ink on top. Depending on the size of the triangles, you can either paint in a thin rectangular panel at either side, as I've done here, or you can paint the triangles right up to the edge of the collar.

four ▷

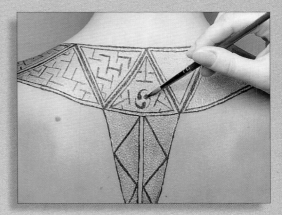

Start at the left-hand side of the collar and paint in the Pictish detail, working inwards from the outer lines of each triangle. Paint in a very basic 'triskele' ('three-limbed' symbol) at the base of the centre triangle, but apart from this don't worry about copying the design precisely, as the overall effect will be the same.

five ▷

Go back to the left-hand side of the design and fill in any large areas with black cosmetic ink. Always leave a bronze line between the block filling and the original line work, and remember to keep a circular shape around the triskele.

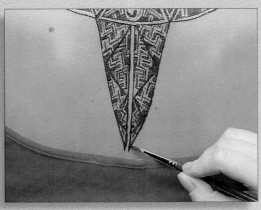

◁ six

Finish off the block filling right down to the tips of the daggers, and then dust the whole design with talcum powder to dry and set it. You now have your very own Celtic body armour! For a variation on this design, why not try painting the collar on its own?

spiral cuff

An effective interlocking design created using repetitive stages

A combination of natural henna and cosmetic dyes has been used for this bold cuff design. It features continuous double-spiral linework – a style dating back thousands of years, commonly found in Celtic spiral patterns. The 'straight-line' spiral echoes the Pictish 'key' style. I've alternated the lines of spirals here, but you could also use the same spiral transfer for the whole cuff if you prefer.

Rub activator into the skin and then apply a thin layer of mehlabiya. To get parallel lines stick tape onto the wrist, leaving equal gaps in between. Then use henna to apply four lines.

▲ **two**

Remove the tape and, if step one took longer than 5 minutes, re-apply mehlabiya oil between the henna lines. Firmly press one of the transfers on the top band, peel, and repeat this process round the band.

spiral cuff

▼ three

Using the other transfer, repeat step two on the central band. Finally, use the same transfer design as in step two to apply the outline to the lower band.

◄ four

Using the henna again, hold the cone near the tip and apply it over the transfer lines. Take care not to smudge any of your work as you go round the arm.

five ►

Finish applying the henna in the final band, remembering to pay close attention to the connecting lines. (If you don't want to apply any dye, your henna design is now complete!)

▼ six

Use a red cosmetic dye to fill in the upper section of the top band. Be careful not to smudge the henna lines that you have just applied.

◀ **seven**

Once you have filled in the top section with the red dye, use a black cosmetic dye to fill in the lower section of the same band.

eight ▶

Repeat this dye application process in the middle band, filling in the red and black dyes as before, and taking care not to move any of the henna linework out of place.

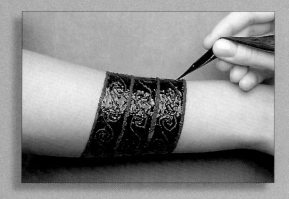

◀ **nine**

Finish the design by filling in the dye on the lower band. Then leave it to dry for around an hour before brushing off the crumbling henna paste and peeling off the dry dye. Avoid contact with water for 12 hours to allow the henna to darken, and use a waterproof spray to prolong the lifespan of the dye.

useful contacts

Established in 1993, Halawa Henna Ltd are the original manufacturers and suppliers of retail and professional henna body art products. Halawa Henna run training courses for professionals and enthusiasts, and now supply a wide range of unique temporary body art products alongside henna. All the products used in this book are available by mail order from Halawa Henna. For further information, contact Halawa Henna Ltd, UK – or a Halawa Henna distributor closer to home. For up-to-date information on products, supply or your nearest professional artist, contact Halawa Henna at the address below or visit their website at www.hennatattoos.com.

UNITED KINGDOM
HALAWA HENNA LTD
96–98 Chapel Street, Leigh
Lancashire WN7 2DB
Tel: (44) 01942 709906
UK freephone 0800 7311160
Fax: (44) 01942 709901
Email: enquires@hennatattoos.com

UNITED STATES
HALAWA HENNA PROFESSIONAL
AND RETAIL DISTRIBUTION
Kathy Rudy
Koolsville, 2639 West Lincoln Avenue
Anaheim, California 92801
Tel: (562) 866 8741
Email: katzkool@aol.com

AUSTRALIA
HALAWA HENNA MAIL-ORDER
DISTRIBUTION
Sandra Ongley
Taking Care of Business
34 Faukland Crescent
Kings Park, 2148 NSW
Tel/Fax: (02) 9837 3100

NEW ZEALAND
HALAWA HENNA PROFESSIONAL AND
RETAIL DISTRIBUTION
Andrew Arkwright
Dome New Zealand
717 Manukau Road, Auckland
PO Box 24   165
New Zealand
Tel/Fax: (09) 625 4921

OTHER SUPPLIERS
A wide range of products is available in high
street stores, but always check that the
products you use are designed to be used
on the skin. Look for an ingredients listing –
if there isn't one, don't buy the product.

Patch test any product first, especially if you
have sensitive skin. Body paints and inks are
readily available from theatre make-up
stores, such as:

CHARLES FOX, 22 Tavistock Street,
Covent Garden, London WC2E 7PY, UK
Tel: 0171 240 3111

KRYOLAN has outlets throughout the
United States. Contact them at the address
below for your nearest stockist.

KRYOLAN CORPORTATION
132 Ninth Street, San Francisco, CA 94103.
Tel (415) 863 9684

further reading

*If you're looking for more
inspiration to create your
own designs, try some of
these books – they're
crammed full of ideas to
help you expand your skills.*

Bain, George. *Celtic Art: The
Methods of Construction.*
London: Constable and Co,
1996. New York: Dover
Publications, 1973
*(Note: this is regarded as
the 'Celtic Design Bible' –
the different styles and*

*construction methods are
illustrated with a vast
selection of actual designs
from numerous reference
sources.)*

Meehan, Aidan. *Celtic
Design: Spiral Patterns.* New
York, London: Thames and
Hudson, 1993

Davis, Courtney. *The Celtic
Art Source Book.* London:
Blandford Press 1989

Marron, Aileen. *Beach Body
Art.* Boston, MA: Journey
Editions, 1999. London:
Piatkus, 1999

Marron, Aileen. *The Henna
Body Art Kit.* Boston, MA:
Journey Editions, 1998.
Toronto: élan press, 1998.
London: Piatkus, 1998.
Sydney: Simon & Schuster,
1998

acknowledgements

AUTHOR'S ACKNOWLEDGEMENTS

I would like to thank Simon Finley, Neil and Wendy Madgwick and Donna Morris for all their support and help, and for putting up with me whilst writing this book!

Thanks to everyone at Eddison Sadd Editions Limited for making it happen, especially Elaine Partington, Liz Wheeler, Tessa Monina, Sophie Bevan and Jamie Hanson, without whose excessive hard work and support this book would not have been possible, and of course the creative talents of Emma Peios.

Extra special thanks to Jeanette and Tony Finley, and Pat and Keith Marron (Mum and Dad), for their on-going support and hard work, and without which Halawa Henna Limited would not exist.

PICTURE CREDITS

The photograph on pages 8–9 is reproduced by kind permission of ET archive.

EDDISON • SADD EDITIONS

Senior Editor Tessa Monina
Commissioning Editor Liz Wheeler
Proofreader Michele Turney
Art Director Elaine Partington
Senior Art Editor Pritty Ramjee
Senior Designer Marissa Feind
Assistant Designer Siu Yin Ho
Photographer Emma Peios
Line artworks Anthony Duke
Production Karyn Claridge and Charles James